The Big Book of
TRAINS

REVISED EDITION

Assistant editor Anwesha Dutta
Assistant art editor Jaileen Kaur
Editor Olivia Stanford
US editor Allison Singer
Project editor Suneha Dutta
Project art editor Yamini Panwar
DTP designer Bimlesh Tiwary
Managing editors Laura Gilbert, Alka Thakur Hazarika
Managing art editors Diane Peyton Jones, Romi Chakraborty
CTS manager Balwant Singh
Production manager Pankaj Sharma
Producer, Pre-production Nadine King
Producer Srijana Gurung
Picture researcher Sakshi Saluja
Art director Martin Wilson
Publisher Sarah Larter
Publishing director Sophie Mitchell
Jacket designers Dheeraj Arora, Kartik Gera
Consultant and additional text Phil Hunt

ORIGINAL EDITION

Editor Jane Yorke
Designer Veneta Altham
Senior managing editor Sarah Phillips
Senior managing art editor Peter Bailey
DTP designer Greg Bryant
Production Josie Alabaster
Jacket design Andrew Nash
Picture researchers James T. Robinson, Christine Rista
Photography Mike Dunning, Richard Leeney
National Railway Museum consultants Christine Heap,
Stephen Hoadley, David Mosley
Railway Museum web address: http://www.nrm.org.uk/

First American Edition, 1998
This edition published in the United States in 2016 by
DK Publishing, 1450 Broadway, Suite 801, New York, NY 10018

Copyright © 1998, 2016 Dorling Kindersley Limited
DK, a Penguin Random House Company LLC

20 10 9 8 7 6
007–294626–Oct/2016

A catalog record for this book is available from the Library of Congress.

ISBN 978-1-4654-5361-7
Printed and bound in China

For the curious

www.dk.com

The publisher would like to thank the following for their kind permission to reproduce their photographs:

(Key: a-above; b-below/bottom; c-center; f-far; l-left; r-right; t-top)
Alamy Images: Alvey & Towers Picture Library 25tr, Andrew Linscott 9tl, Bildarchiv Monheim GmbH 29tl,
Dave Porter 24clb, David R. Frazier Photolibrary, Inc. 11tr, Iain Masterton 22-23, imageBROKER 28t, John
Elk III 21cr, JTB Media Creation, Inc. 14-15, 23t, Malcolm Fairman 23br, Mark Hicken 10-11b, Martin Bond
24-25, mediacolor's 2cr, 12-13, Olaf Protze 31cr, peter jordan 18-19, picturesbyrob 9tr, qaphotos.com 16-17,
17tl, 19cra, Rick Pisio\RWP Photography 1, 3cra, 6-7, robertharding 14tl, Stefano Politi Markovina 29c,
STOCKFOLIO® 20-21, Sylvain Oliveira 20tr, Universal Images Group North America LLC / DeAgostini 15tl;
Corbis: Colin Garratt / Milepost 92 1 / 2 19tl, Gerhard Kraus / imageBROKER 30-31, Ian Cumming / Design
Pics 18tl, John Harper 2tr, 4b, Steve Crise / Transtock 12ca; **David Hennessey:** 30tl; **Dorling Kindersley:**
Mike Dunning / National Railway Museum, York 3b, 4cla, 8-9, Museum of Transportation, St Louis, Missouri
10-11t, Science Museum, London / Science Museum, London 2br, 4cra, The Science Museum, London 2crb,
3crb, 5; **Dreamstime.com:** Americanspirit 29b, Christa Eder 26cr, David Watmough 8tr, Languste 1 (Train),
6c, Sean Pavone 22tr, Thomas Vieth 12clb, Typhoonski 24cla, Yinglina 21tl; **Getty Images:** Bloomberg 17cra,
Hiroyuki Nagaoka 26tr, Mike Danneman 31tr, Olaf Protze / LightRocket 26bl, Schöning / ullstein bild 27

All other images © Dorling Kindersley
For further information see: www.dkimages.com

Contents

Early steam locomotives

In Britain, the first railroads were built to carry coal, and horses were used to pull the open freight cars along. In 1804, Richard Trevithick built the first steam locomotive, but it was slower than a horse and so heavy that it kept breaking the track. Soon people were making reliable steam locomotives that could carry goods and passengers quickly over longer distances.

This cutaway replica of *Rocket* enables you to see inside the boiler

The tender carried coke for fuel. Water was carried in the barrel

First-class passenger cars were similar to stagecoaches

First railroad

Rocket worked on the Liverpool and Manchester Railway, opened in 1830. It was the first railroad to provide passenger trains pulled by steam locomotives.

Rocket locomotive

Rocket was designed by Robert Stephenson in 1829. This 5-ton (4.5 metric ton) steam locomotive was successful because the design used all the latest ideas. It could travel at speeds of up to 25 mph (40 kph) on its intercity journey.

Exhaust steam went up the tall smokestack

The boiler heated water to make steam

The fireman shoveled coke into the firebox. The heat from the fire passed along tubes inside the boiler

The driver and fireman stood on a small platform

The steam pushed the pistons, and the connecting rods turned the wheels

huge cylinders that
~~ntained~~ the pistons were
~~ight~~ on this engine

Puffing Billy took its name
from the loud noise made
by the exhaust steam

Transporting coal

Puffing Billy is one of the oldest
surviving steam locomotives. It
was built in England in 1813, to
a design by William Hedley. The
locomotive worked for 48 years on a railroad
just 5 miles (8 km) long. It pulled coal cars at
walking pace from Wylam coal mine to a
nearby river for transportation by barge.

The pistons made the beams
rock backward and forward.
These moved the connecting
rods, which turned the wheels

The boiler produced steam,
which entered the cylinders
and pushed the pistons

The tender
carried the coke
fuel supply

The connecting rods
moved cogs, which
turned the wheels

The locomotive ran on
cast-iron, "fish-bellied"
rails. These had a
thicker midsection
for added strength

5

American steam locomotives

Railroads soon spread all over the world, carrying people and goods faster than anything else had before. The first railroad built across the United States of America was finished in May 1869. Colorful steam locomotives, like the ones shown here, carried settlers traveling to the new towns in the west. These locomotives were called 4-4-0s, because they had four driving wheels and four bogie wheels to guide the engine on the sometimes poor track. The bogie could swivel from side to side around the twisting tracks.

The smokestack let out smoke and used steam

A large, powerful oil lamp warned people that a train was coming at night

Door into the smokebox

119

Wood-burning locomotive

Jupiter was an early American locomotive that burned wood for fuel. This famous engine worked on the Central Pacific Railroad. It had a large funnel-shaped smokestack to catch the shower of sparks that came out of the engine with the smoke and steam.

The cowcatcher was a strong, metal grid that protected the locomotive from coming off the track if it hit a buffalo on the line

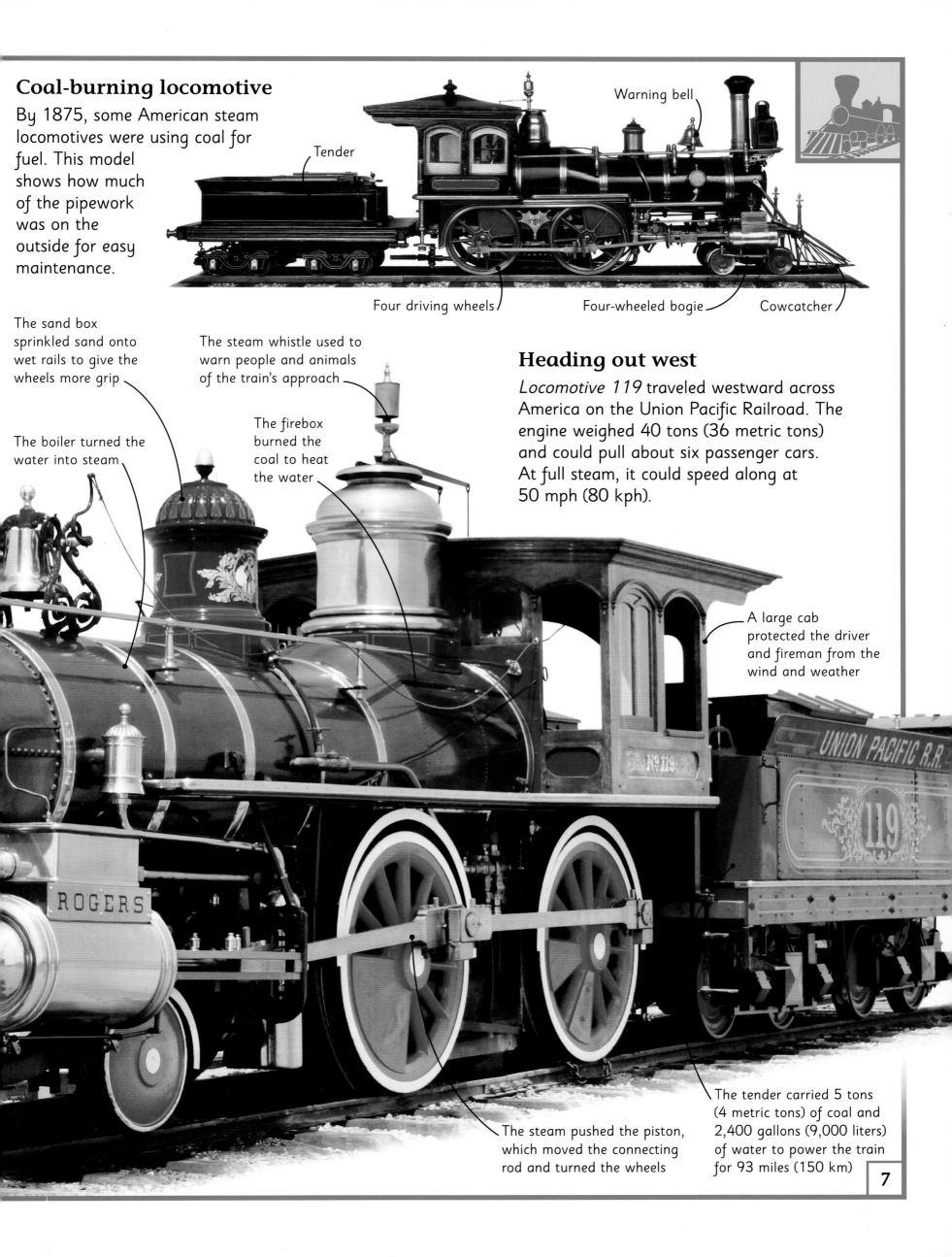

Coal-burning locomotive

By 1875, some American steam locomotives were using coal for fuel. This model shows how much of the pipework was on the outside for easy maintenance.

Warning bell

Tender

Four driving wheels

Four-wheeled bogie

Cowcatcher

The sand box sprinkled sand onto wet rails to give the wheels more grip

The steam whistle used to warn people and animals of the train's approach

The firebox burned the coal to heat the water

The boiler turned the water into steam

Heading out west

Locomotive 119 traveled westward across America on the Union Pacific Railroad. The engine weighed 40 tons (36 metric tons) and could pull about six passenger cars. At full steam, it could speed along at 50 mph (80 kph).

A large cab protected the driver and fireman from the wind and weather

ROGERS

UNION PACIFIC R.R

119

The steam pushed the piston, which moved the connecting rod and turned the wheels

The tender carried 5 tons (4 metric tons) of coal and 2,400 gallons (9,000 liters) of water to power the train for 93 miles (150 km)

Fast steam locomotives

Some passenger trains, called express trains, are designed to run nonstop between two cities. In the 1930s, the finest steam locomotives ever built pulled such trains. Some had sleek, streamlined shapes to help them go faster, and bigger engines that could run for long periods at speeds of more than 99 mph (160 kph).

Large cylinders make the engine very powerful

Buffers help prevent damage to the locomotive

Fastest steam locomotive

Mallard holds the unbeaten record as the fastest steam locomotive in the world. On July 3, 1938, it reached a speed of 126 mph (202 kph) running downhill between Grantham and Peterborough, in England. This speed record was set during the trials of brake equipment on the streamlined cars of the London and North Eastern Railway.

Locomotive engineer

This locomotive is an A4 Class, the same type as *Mallard*. It is named *Sir Nigel Gresley*, after the mechanical engineer who designed the engines.

The driver and fireman operated the locomotive from the footplate

These rods drove a very accurate speedometer

The smokebox door can be opened to clean the soot out of the front of the engine

Famous express train

Flying Scotsman is one of the most famous locomotives in the world. In 1928, it headed the first nonstop express train from London to Edinburgh, in Scotland—a distance of 413 miles (665 km). On its daily run in 1934, the train set a speed record for steam locomotives of 100 mph (161 kph).

The specially designed double smokestack let out steam and smoke efficiently

Mallard can be seen on display at the National Railway Museum in England

Train attraction

Flying Scotsman is still kept in working order today, so that passengers can enjoy traveling on a train pulled by this very famous locomotive.

The streamlined nose and engine casing helped the locomotive travel at high speeds

MALLARD

The engine weighed 182 tons (165 metric tons) and was more than 69 ft (21 m) long

Mallard was a 4-6-2 locomotive. It had four leading wheels, six large 7-ft (2-m) driving wheels, and two trailing wheels

Powerful steam locomotives

By the 1940s, engineers were designing bigger and more powerful steam engines to pull heavy freight trains at higher speeds. These huge locomotives often had two sets of cylinders and driving wheels under one very large boiler. They were called articulated engines because the driving wheels could pivot under the boiler to travel around tight bends.

Big Boy weighed 254 tons (230 metric tons)

The two sets of four massive driving wheels each measured 5½ ft (1.7 m) in diameter

Water for the boiler was carried in this tank at the front of the engine

The heavy engine could pull 1,543 tons (1,400 metric tons) of freight

African freight

From 1954, the 20A Class Garratt locomotive hauled loads of coal and copper in the countries now called Zambia and Zimbabwe. This articulated locomotive had engine units at the front and back, with the boiler slung between them. The design enabled the powerful locomotive to travel around bends on lightweight tracks in the African bush. Despite the train being heavy, it didn't topple over.

The brake pipes ran the entire length of the train and enabled the driver to control all of the train vehicles

Biggest steam locomotive

America's Union Pacific Railroad built 25 *Big Boy* locomotives between 1941 and 1944, based on an idea by Anatole Mallet. These monster engines were 131 ft (40 m) long and 16 ft (5 m) high. They had 16 driving wheels and could travel at 80 mph (130 kph).

The cowcatcher prevented animals on the track from becoming trapped under the locomotive

American giant

At 121 ft (37 m) long, *The Challenger* was the *Big Boy*'s little cousin. The engine had 12 driving wheels and was used to haul passenger and goods trains over the Rocky Mountains and across the western deserts.

The large boiler supplied steam to the two power units

The bunker and tank held 9,510 gallons (36,000 liters) of water and 28 tons (25 metric tons) of coal

The front engine unit had four leading wheels, eight driving wheels, and two trailing wheels

Freight trains

Today's cleaner, diesel-electric locomotives have replaced the powerful steam locomotives of the past. These modern engines can haul large amounts of freight over long distances using less fuel than trucks would need. They transport all sorts of goods—food produce like wheat and eggs, coal for industry, cars, and even tanks!

The locomotive runs at a top speed of 62 mph (100 kph)

Long-haul journeys

The Santa Fe diesel-electric locomotive is used to haul freight more than 2,200 miles (3,541 km) across the USA, from California to Chicago. The large fuel tanks keep the engines going on the long desert runs.

Huge tanks carry up to 462 gallons (1,750 liters) of diesel fuel

The driver enters the cab using the steps and a door in the front of the locomotive

The air brakes act directly on the wheels to stop the train safely

The small snowplow can clear snowdrifts or debris off the line

Pulling power

This heavy freight train crossing the deserts of Arizona is hauled by four diesel engines, operated by just one driver. The whole train is around 3 miles (4.8 km) long. Behind the locomotives, there are five double-decker freight cars. The following 80 or more cars carry freight in large containers, loaded in a "piggyback" style.

Locomotive identification number

The driver's cab is fully protected against the weather

Powerful freight locomotive

This freight locomotive of the Santa Fe Railroad is 49 ft (15 m) long and weighs 123 tons (112 metric tons). Diesel oil fuels the engine that generates electricity to drive the wheels.

The 12 driving wheels are powered by electric motors

13

Long train journeys

Some train journeys take days to complete. The trains are equipped with everything that the passengers need to spend a long time onboard. There are cars with seats for use in the day, and sleeping cars with beds where travelers can spend the night. Meals are served in a restaurant car.

Observation carriages

The Canadian Pacific Railway attaches special observation cars with viewing domes at the end of its trains. The upper-level seats enable passengers to get a good view of the spectacular scenery as they travel through the Rocky Mountains.

Ventilator grilles allow air in to cool the diesel engines. These drive the electric generators, which power the electric motors

Two locomotives are used for extra pulling power where there are steep hills

Crossing Canada

A journey on the Canadian Trans-Continental takes three days from Vancouver to Toronto, a distance of 2,771 miles (4,459 km). The train is long and heavy with up to 19 cars. It is pulled by a large, powerful diesel locomotive running at a top speed of 103 mph (166 kph).

The train has a luggage car, which also includes living quarters for the train crew

Electric motors turn the locomotive's wheels

The large fuel tanks allow the locomotive to travel long distances before refueling

Longest train journey

It takes eight days to travel on the Trans-Siberian Express from Moscow to Vladivostok in Russia. The line is 5,766 miles (9,279 km) long, and the train stops at 70 stations along the way. This makes it the longest train journey in the world without changing trains.

The driver climbs up steps into the driving cab. From here, the driver gets a good view of the line ahead

Wipers are essential for clearing snow and rain from the windshield

The strong headlights let people see the train coming

6446

6446

6446

GPA-30c

VIA

Channel Tunnel trains *Le Shuttle*

The Channel Tunnel is 31 miles (50 km) long and runs under the English Channel, linking the railroads of France and England. Special electric trains have been running through the tunnel since 1994. *Le Shuttle* is the service that transports cars, buses, and trucks, with a fleet of over 50 electric locomotives making the 35-minute journey to France.

Car transporter

Le Shuttle trains make about 20 journeys every day between the coastal towns of Folkestone in southern England and Calais in northern France. They carry cars and buses under the sea, rather than over it by ferry. The vehicle carriers can be loaded with up to 120 cars, 12 buses, and 1,000 passengers, who stay in their vehicles during the journey. The trains have a locomotive at each end – the back one pushes and the front one pulls. Freight trucks travel on their own shuttle trains.

The train weighs up to 2,646 tons (2,400 metric tons) and is 2,461 ft (750 m) long

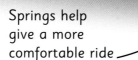

EURO TUNNEL

9012

901

Springs help give a more comfortable ride

Sand is carried in this box and blown onto the rails to give the wheels more grip in wet weather

Inside the driver's cab

The cabin of *Le Shuttle* contains many lights, switches, and screens to assist the driver. It was designed without side windows to help the driver focus on the track ahead. The train's speed is controlled by computer, which also reads the signals along the line.

The driver sits on the left in the front cab

Loud air horns are hidden behind this grille, which allows air in to cool the engine

The driver sits on the right in the cab at the rear

Electric power

Le Shuttle is powered by electricity collected from an overhead wire and has a top speed of 99 mph (160 kph). There are backup batteries on board, so the train's systems can still operate if the power supply fails.

The locomotive at the back of the train has red taillights

Air brake pipes and couplings allow the locomotive to be joined to another train if it breaks down

Channel Tunnel trains *Eurostar*

The *Eurostar* is another train that runs through the Channel Tunnel between England and France. Unlike *Le Shuttle*, it only carries passengers, on a dedicated high-speed line that enables people to travel from London to Paris in only two hours and 15 minutes, or to Brussels in under two hours. The network is always expanding, and as well as recent new routes to the south of France, there are also plans for a direct service to Amsterdam.

St Pancras International station

Eurostar trains have their own specially built platforms at St Pancras International Station, in London. Just like at airports, international passengers go through passport checks in the Eurostar departure lounge before boarding their train.

Eurostar's yellow paintwork makes the train more visible

Eurostar is 1,115 ft (340 m) long. It has a locomotive at each end and 20 passenger cars

Passengers can buy refreshments from the on-board buffet service

Passenger train

The *Eurostar* trains are similar to French TGV trains with a top speed of 186 mph (300 kph). Thanks to the Channel Tunnel, they can carry 800 passengers between London and Paris, or Brussels in Belgium, in about two hours. It also connects London to Lyon, Avignon, and Marseilles. These high-speed trains are very complex because they have to run on the railroads of three different countries.

Ventilator grilles let in air to cool down the electrical equipment

The train gathers electricity from the overhead wire with its pantograph, or from a third rail on the ground with this special pickup

Eurostar in Britain

In France, Belgium, and Britain, *Eurostar* travels on special high-speed lines. The British high-speed line was the last to be completed, and trains started running on it in 2007.

The driver looks out through the small windshield

Powerful headlights warn of the train's approach

Underwater journey

It takes about 30 minutes for a train to travel through the Channel Tunnel. There are, in fact, three tunnels dug 148 ft (45 m) below the seabed. Trains run in opposite directions in the two large tunnels, on either side of a smaller, safety access tunnel.

3101

The coupling is behind these doors

The skirt and nose of the train are streamlined for high-speed running

TGVs

The *Train à Grande Vitesse*, or TGV, is France's high-speed electric train. It came into service in 1981, running on special tracks between Paris and Lyon. In 1990, an improved TGV *Atlantique* linked Paris and Bordeaux, and today many other French cities are connected by TGV lines. The locomotives can reach 186 mph (300 kph), though one modified TGV has set the world-record speed of over 357 mph (574 kph).

Intercity passenger train

The high-speed, gray-and-blue TGV *Atlantique* is an impressive sight. The train has a refreshment car, three first-class cars, and six second-class cars, which together carry a full load of 500 passengers.

Locomotives at both ends

All TGVs have a powerful electric motor unit, or engine, attached to the front and back of the train. The nose has antennae that pick up signals from the tracks for the driver.

The locomotive's eight driving wheels are powered by electric motors

The pantograph picks up
electricity from overhead wires

Computer controls

When traveling at top speeds, it takes
the TGV around 1.8 miles (3 km) to stop
safely. The braking and signaling systems
are controlled by a computer in the
driver's cab. This TGV *Duplex* has
a double-decker seating layout.

The TGV runs at its fastest on
a growing network of special
tracks. It can use ordinary tracks
but has to run at slower speeds

The streamlined
body helps the train
travel at high speeds

Fast ride

Riding in the TGV is very
comfortable even at high speeds.
Passengers are able to eat a meal,
use their phones, or watch
a movie on the train.

The nose is
packed with
signaling
antennae

The skirt stops things
from being trapped
underneath the train

Bullet trains

The futuristic-looking, high-speed electric trains that run in Japan are called bullet trains. Their Japanese name is *Shinkansen*. When they were introduced in 1964, the trains provided the first passenger service in the world to travel at speeds of 100 mph (161 kph). Today, the trains reach much faster speeds of up to 199 mph (320 kph), running on specially designed tracks. Bullet trains also offer very frequent service, and carry nearly one million passengers every day.

Speeding past Mount Fuji

Modern bullet trains are made of aluminum alloy for speed and to save weight. This *Tokaido Shinkansen* travels from Tokyo to Osaka, which is the world's most traveled high-speed train line. It has transported more than 5.3 billion passengers.

High-speed journey

The N700 bullet train has a top speed of 186 mph (300 kph). It has cut the journey time from Tokyo to Osaka, a distance of 321 miles (516 km), to 2 hours and 20 minutes.

The driver sits high up and has a clear view of the line ahead

The streamlined nose helps it run along at high speeds

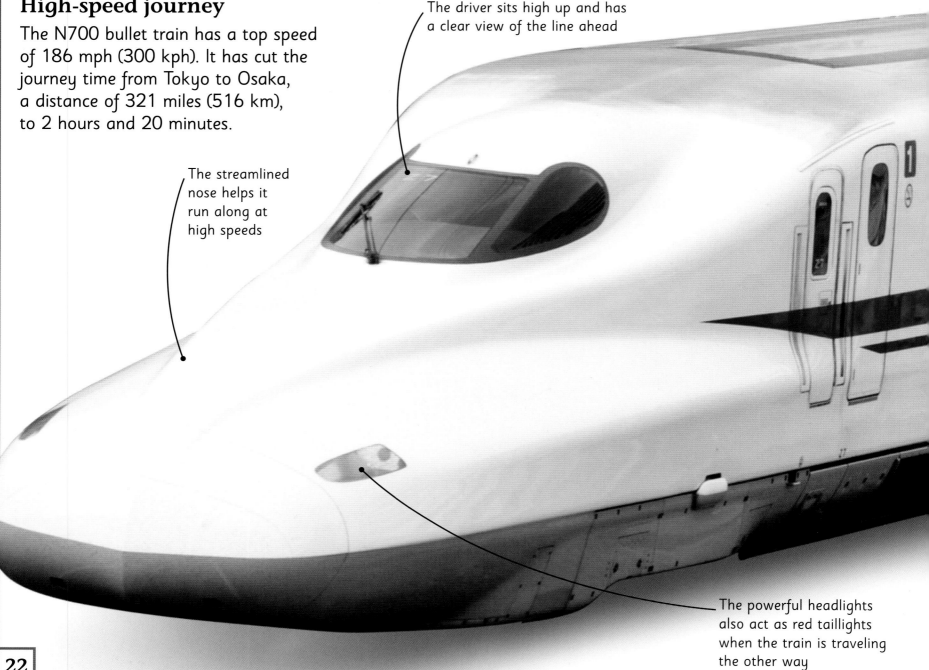

The powerful headlights also act as red taillights when the train is traveling the other way

The windows are small, like those of an airplane

The front of the train is ultra-streamlined for travel at very high speeds

E6 series

The E6 series is a high-speed bullet train launched in 2013. It has seven cars that carry passengers from Tokyo to Akita and to Aomori. The Tokyo–Aomori route is 420 miles (676 km) long and is the longest bullet train route. The elongated nose helps it achieve a top speed of 199 mph (320 kph).

The trains have up to 16 cars and carry 1,300 passengers

A 300 series *Shinkansen*, dating from 1993

The 100 series *Shinkansen* has been running since 1986

This *Shinkansen* was one of the first trains introduced in 1964

The 700 series has been operating since 1999

Bullet train designs

Since their introduction over 50 years ago, bullet trains have constantly been redesigned to further reduce air resistance, increasing travel speeds.

High-speed passenger trains

Trains are now running at faster and faster speeds, because they have to compete with cars and airplanes for passengers traveling between major cities. High-speed passenger trains run on electric power picked up from overhead lines. Some countries have built brand-new railroad networks for their fast electric trains. Others run a high-speed service on existing tracks and fit the trains into their normal rail schedules.

Head- or taillights are used, depending on which way the train is traveling

Fast and slow tracks

Germany's high-speed trains run on both existing tracks and newly built lines. The ICE electric engines can only run at their top speed of 186 mph (300 kph) when traveling on the new lines.

The power car and other cars are made of tough molded plastic

England to Scotland

This InterCity 125 runs between London and Scotland and has a top speed of 125 mph (201 kph). It is the fastest diesel locomotive in the world.

The lip on the power car acts as a small snowplow

Tilting train

The railroads of Sweden are all twists and turns. The engine and cars of the X2000 train tilt when going round corners. This enables the train to keep up its top speed of 124 mph (200 kph).

The train has a driving car at both ends, which makes it possible to depart right away on the return trip

The pantograph picks up electric power from overhead wires

The X2000 power car pulls five passenger cars on its intercity journeys

Traveling on straight lines

The Italian ETR 500 can travel at 186 mph (300 kph). It runs on specially built high-speed routes with few curves. This means that the train can maintain its fast speed without slowing down for bends or other traffic on the line.

Mountain trains

Railroads are very popular in mountainous areas where it would be difficult to build a road. Many mountain railroads were built so that people could enjoy the view from the train. Rack railroads have special tracks that can run up the sides of mountains. Under the engine, the train has a powered cogwheel, which grips a toothed rail. This allows the train to climb very steep slopes and prevents it from slipping backward.

World's highest railroad

Completed in 2006, the Quinghai–Lhasa route in China features the world's highest railroad line. At the Tanggula Pass in western China, the track is 16,640 ft (5,072 m) above sea level.

Tourist train

The Brienz–Rothorn train is now a tourist attraction. This rack railroad is 4.6 miles (7.5 km) long and is the only one in Switzerland that still uses steam locomotives. Powerful engines push the passenger cars up the mountainside, to a height of 5,512 ft (1,680 m).

The passenger cars are pushed uphill by the steam locomotive

A cogged wheel on the engine climbs up the toothed rack

The locomotive is built at an angle so that it stays level on the steep slope

Bridges and tunnels

Railroads in mountainous areas have to use many bridges, viaducts, and tunnels to pass through difficult terrain. This train is called the *Glacier Express* because it runs through deep snow for many months of the year. It carries passengers to ski resorts in the Swiss mountains.

Steepest rack railroad

The Mount Pilatus Railway in Switzerland is the steepest rack railroad in the world. The railroad used steam engines when it was opened in 1889, but electric trains took over in 1937. The trains are single cars and have a top speed of 5.6 mph (9 kph).

The cars are specially designed so that the passenger seats match the angle of the slope

The pantograph collects electricity from the wires running overhead

Trains travel up and down the mountain on the same track

The rack is laid between the ordinary rails

Rails run in both directions

The train is powered by electric motors

Giant, steel legs support the monorail track

342

341

340

Monorail

These special trains hang or balance on a single rail, called a monorail. The trains have motors, which are powered by electricity. Monorail trains run high up off the ground and carry passengers across busy cities, traveling over the tops of roads, buildings, and rivers. Riding on a monorail seems like flying and can be very exciting.

Hanging train

The Wuppertal monorail, in Germany, is built over a river. The hanging cars are like an ordinary train, but the driving wheels are on the roof. The stations are at the same level as the track. Passengers reach the platforms by escalator.

Avoiding the busy traffic

People use the Wuppertal monorail like a bus to travel to work, or to go shopping. Some children even go to school on it.

The wide windshield gives the driver a clear, all-round view

The train cars straddle the concrete track

Sliding doors let the passengers in and out at stations

Monorails for fun

Some monorails, like the Seattle Expo Alweg, are built to take visitors around a large exhibition or amusement park. The cars have big windows so everyone can see outside and get a good view. Monorails usually only have one or two cars, which can carry up to 100 people.

The wheels run along the top of the rail and take the train's weight. Guide wheels run along the sides to keep the train balanced

Four cars accommodate a total of 72 seated and 152 standing passengers

Transporting tourists

The Las Vegas Monorail runs in Nevada. It can travel at a speed of 50 mph (80 kph). It is 3.9 miles (6.3 km) long and transports tourists along a seven-station line behind the Las Vegas Strip.

Snow trains

When railroad lines become blocked by snow, special trains are needed to dig out the tracks so that trains can start running again. Snowplows can be used to clear deep snowdrifts, but in really severe conditions, rotary snowblowers are needed to open up the line. These snow trains were first used in the USA in 1869.

Diesel power

This British snow train is diesel-powered and does not need a locomotive to push it. Large blades break up the snow, which is then blown clear of the track. Deep snow is rare in Britain, so the train is stored in a depot when not in use.

Steam snowblower

This snowblower worked on the railroads of Alaska, and was powered by steam. It had a crew of three—the fireman, the engineer who looked after the machinery, and the pilot who signaled to the "pusher" locomotives.

Boiler car, from where the pilot observed the snowy track ahead

This vehicle contained equipment and facilities for the crew

The tender carried the coal and water to fuel the boiler

Narrow-gauge wheels ran on the White Pass and Yukon Railway

Snowblower at work

This steam-powered snowblower clears the tracks by cutting into the snowdrift and then blowing the loose snow away from the line. The train can clear about 131 ft (40 m) of deep snow per minute. It is moved along the line by "pusher" locomotives.

The powerful headlight could light up the track in blizzard conditions

Loose snow was broken up by the wheel, blown out of this chute, and thrown clear of the track

Large side blades sliced a path through the snowdrifts and channeled the snow into the spinning wheel

Clearing tracks

Snowblowers clear the line before other trains start running. In very heavy snowstorms, they may be needed to rescue stranded trains.

The snowblower was powered by steam from a boiler inside the blower

The giant spinning wheel broke up the snow

Glossary

bogie Set of four wheels fitted under a locomotive or wagon to help it turn on a curved track

boiler Large metal drum on a steam locomotive, where the water is turned into steam

car Carriages that carry passengers on a train

coke Type of coal used as fuel for early steam locomotives

connecting rod Metal rod that links the piston to the driving wheels of a steam locomotive

coupling Device for joining cars to an engine and to each other to form a train

cylinder Metal tube in which steam or gas under pressure pushes the piston to drive the wheels

diesel-electric engine Locomotive using diesel oil as the fuel to generate electricity, which in turn powers electric motors that drive the wheels

driving wheels Main wheels that are connected to a power supply and move a locomotive

electric engine Locomotive powered by electricity picked up from an electric cable or third rail

firebox Metal box behind a steam locomotive's boiler, where the fuel is burned

fireman Person on a steam engine who shovels coal into the firebox and keeps the boiler topped up with water

footplate Driver's cab on a steam engine

locomotive Vehicle at the front or rear of a train that provides the power to move it

pantograph Metal frame on top of an electric locomotive, that picks up electricity from cables hanging above the track

power car Diesel or electric locomotive permanently joined to a set of passenger cars

tender Carriage containing coal to power a steam train

third rail Rail on the ground that supplies electricity to some electric trains

viaduct Long, high bridge, supported by huge columns, built over a valley or river

wagon Train vehicles that carries freight, or goods

Index